Leaf and Stone

Margaret West

Margaret West was born in 1936 in Melbourne, her formal studies include art, music and philosophy. In 1979 she moved to Sydney, where she taught art theory and practice at Sydney University College of the Arts from 1979 to 1999. She has travelled, exhibited, and lectured extensively in Australia and overseas and her work is represented in major public national and international art collections. Her essays, and poetry are published in anthologies, journals and catalogues. She has also (self)published several artist's books which develop a dialogue between text and image. Her work is broadly informed by interests which range through art, literature, music, philosophy, science and technology. The metaphoric potential of the everyday world and concern about political issues provide grist to her mill. Since 2000 Margaret West has lived in Blackheath in the Upper Blue Mountains of New South Wales, where she works full time as an artist and writer.

PREVIOUS PUBLICATIONS

limited edition artist books of words and images
Sketches: Ashfield Park
'scape
In Lieu of Flowers
Magnolias, Wonder, Doubt

Leaf and Stone

Margaret West

Brandl & Schlesinger

Text copyright © Margaret West, 2012
Cover drawing: *Song of the Winds* © Margaret West, 2012
Drawings © Margaret West, 2012

All rights reserved. Without limiting the rights under copyright reserved above,
apart from any fair dealing for the purpose of criticism, review, research,
no part of this publication may be reproduced, stored in or introduced into
a retrieval system, or transmitted, in any form or by any means (electronic,
mechanical, photocopying, recording or otherwise), without the prior written
permission of both the copyright owner and the publisher of this book.

First published in 2012
by Brandl & Schlesinger
www.brandl.com.au

Book design: Andras Berkes-Brandl

This project has been assisted by the Commonwealth Government through the
Australia Council, its arts funding and advisory body.

National Library of Australia Cataloguing-in-Publication entry:
Author: West, Margaret.
Title: Leaf and stone / Margaret West.
ISBN: 978-1-921556-32-6 (pbk)
Dewey Number: A821.4

Printed and bound by Trojan Press, Melbourne

Acknowledgements

Previously published poems:
'Have you Heard?' in *Australian Book Review*, June 2001
'After a walk to the frog pond', 'Allow me this', 'Poppies',
'Eleven Black Pansies' (as 'Dark Thoughts'), 'Spring', and 'The tacit
truth of stone', in *Magnolias, Wonder, Doubt*, Margaret West, 2003
'Present in the morning', and 'Raven', in *'scape*, Margaret West 2003
'Sketches from a Garden' in the exhibition *Words and Things*,
Studio 20/17, Sydney, 2011.

My thanks to Veronica Sumegi and Andras Berkes of Brandl and
Schlesinger for their accomplished and generous support in the
development of this book, to Gail Jones for the constancy of her
friendship and warm expression of her belief in my work,
and to David West for his loving kindness.

Contents

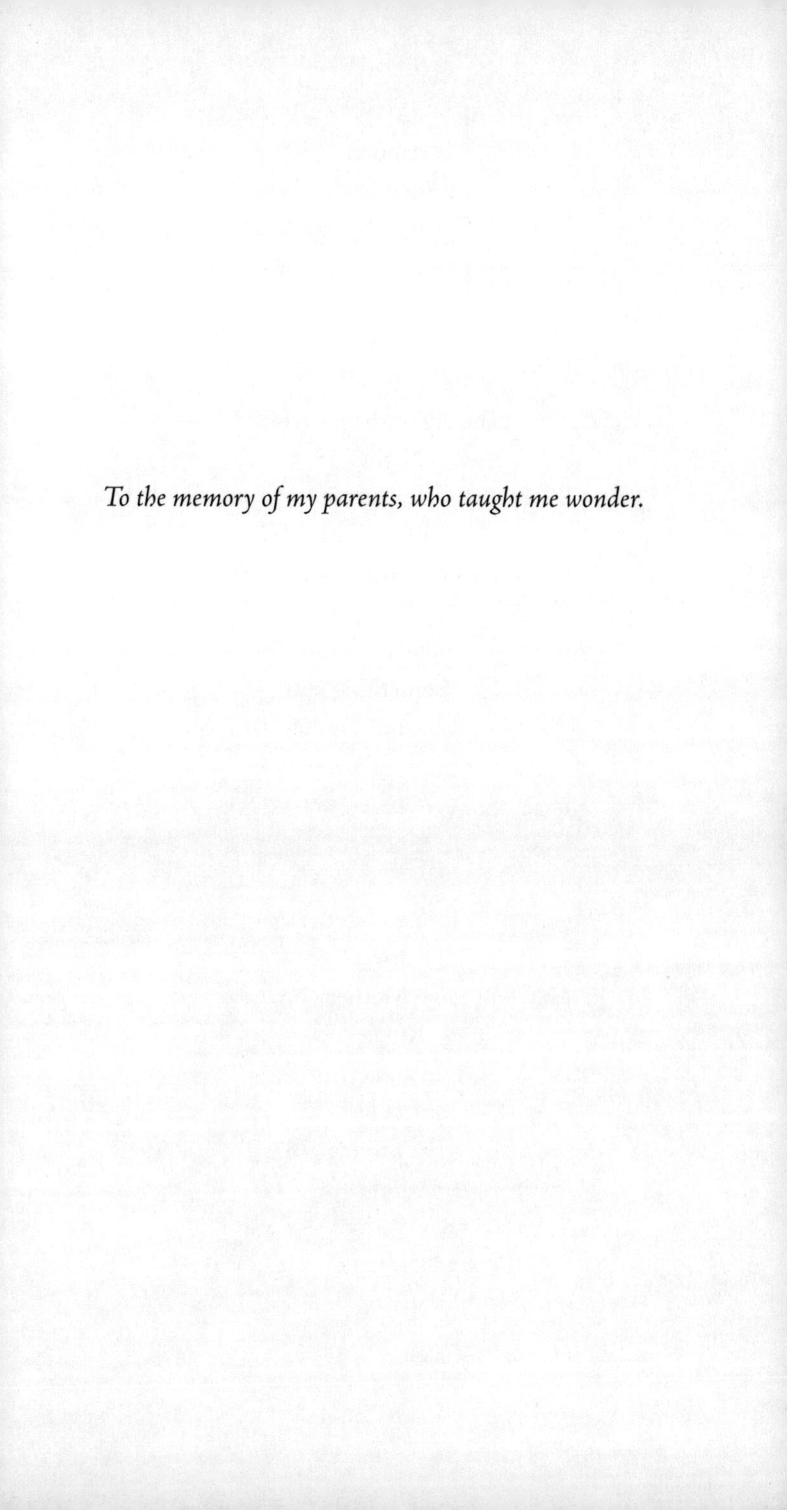

To the memory of my parents, who taught me wonder.

There are words

There are words for things
that fall

    petals
        (cheeks
         and faces)
    leaves
        (in extremis)
    drops
    and flakes

    wings
        (smudged with wax)
    arches
    angels

    all
on an in-breath of earth

HYACINTH

I wrote HYACINTH
this morning, watched Y follow H, A follow Y,
then C, and I, N, T;
watched to the last H my haptic glyphs. Watched
plant emerge from pen.

Without the word, can I have it
as would a dog, bird, bee,
an earthworm?

There are other words: globular, pale, pointed, writhe,
shoot, green, burst, then blue or pink or white: an image
begins to emerge but when I close my eyes
I cannot inhale those words as I can
                HYACINTH
                    HYACINTH
                        HYACINTH

Remarks on Yellow

If it were red we could talk
of the earth oozing blood
of the young fed to canons — of their surrogate
the poppies' flagrant splash.
If blue, the sky
would be invoked, or discreet sprinkles
of forget-me-nots. Green
would merely dissolve in green-ness.
But how to tag hectares of rape
screaming at the sky or the shrieks
of coreopsis bound to railway-tracks
on summer nights?

These words

What   is a rock?
          is a cave?
                    A tree
is man or woman.
                    The earth
breathes these words:
          rock

          cave

          tree

          man

          woman

          (breathe
me, breathe
you)
                    The growth
on our heads mingles (the roots
are white.
                    Flesh once
embarked on such
a venture.)
                    A progeny
of saplings is caught too
briefly in the soft cage of its
limbs,
                    slides
beyond the edge of
our knowing.

       The leaves
of our hands flail
in vain.
       What
is a rock
is a cave
are these
      words?

Words

My friend the geologist, who is sure,
tells me stone is a substance
and (a) rock is a thing, though some end up
rounder than rock which rolls
to begin, but finishes with that
blasted "ck", whereas stone is both
obdurate and smoothly worn.
Now boulders sound
smoother and rounder than shoulders
and cobbles
which may be soft as an egg
and round as your arms round
me, speak ruggedly, twist
tongues and ankles. Pebbles
meddle playfully in the overrun
and gravel crunches mincely in the mouth,
feigning propriety, alerting
nights and causing
a hasty rash. Sand
runs through hands, speaks
grittily, scratches eyes and scours
or burns the soles of utterance. Clay
slips.

After *The Mustard Seed Garden*

After *The Mustard Seed Garden** you saw the world
in brush-strokes — the trunks
of trees bore their dark load
aloft in rising sweeps, young leaves flicked
verdure off new-found
fingers, and grasses swished darkly inscribing
wind across the pallid face of morning.

At night a graffiti of beetles clicked
questions of inflection, weight, tempo; and moths —
sleek, spreadeagled, or deltoid — splotched their soft
ink in silhouette across the window, blotted
and smudged walls; and the brush
outdid the world.

And the rain? What are the rules
for rain? Water from sky as gravity
or ink decree, plashing disturbingly on pool
or page; the slant of rain is clear, drawn
down from cloud to earth   from right
to left, or left to right according the rule
of wind (or measured in its gauge — delineated,
calibrated,
metricated)
     And mist?
There is no mark, no point, no single
brush-borne fine-inked

hair to spell obscurity and silence. The blank of world
or page awaits
                              awaits
                                    awaits

Now drops hang on the verandah rail pending
instruction — each an infinity of light, a universe
minute and trembling with close scrutiny
and breath.   They hold.   They hold.

Where can we learn the brush-stroke
of their fall?

★ Chieh Tzu Yüan Hua Chuan (1679-1701). *The Mustard Seed Garden
Manual of Painting.* Translated by Mai-mai Sze. Princeton University Press,
Bollingen, 1956.

Shhh!

Something about lollipop pink sets me craving
black and the screeching claw and flutter of fruit
bats drives me into the light like the kid-scuffling school-
holiday scrum at the gallery bistro drove me to anticipate
tranquillity here in the gardens but bats and the shrill
of lollipoppins drown peace in skreak and shriek
and bubble and squeak.
      Shhh!

      You can almost hear the water
course, the tattered stalking of the ibis, the brown
of bobbing ducks.
          A deep woman squats on the path
before a small, pale leaf — hands spread,
nose to the gravel, legs high in a purple frog-kick
her bare heels brush her satin rump. A chopper
hacks at the sky and an ashen blond in azure preens (Yes!)
I sit — all ballpoint eyes and ears. Violetta perches
on the bridge — a neighing greying bare-foot child —
bells on her ankles and rings on her toes.
I put on my black jacket, pay the bill and run
the shades of shrieking bats.

Allow me this

I call the small
discarded plastic

disc a flower.
Allow me this.

They are too complex
radiant,

sumptuous
glorious

too floral in their
efflorescence, too

petalled, bifurcated,
crenellated, variegated

nectared, honeyed
pollinated

too red too white too pink too yellow
orange

too bee-ed, too butter-flown
too growing, grown

too dewed
too sunned

too watched by moon
too matched by stars

too breathing
breathed upon

too sniffed
too petal cheeked

too pert, languorous
poisonous, amorous

too intoxicating
too asphyxiating

full-faced they
watch too much

and are too budding,
bursting

fading,
wilting

drooping
dropping

too decaying
and too fast-forward

too much promise
and too much humus.

They are too sweet
with death.

So allow me this.
Picked

from the macadam
a spare flower

or any stone
obdurate

irrevocable as
a purple

small and
plastic disc.

In search of Yoghourt

On my early morning
walk in search of yoghourt
and poetry I found
signs on the road
from last night's storm.

I found a man in grey shorts
whisking leaf glyphs from his drive
left   right   left   right
muttering responses.

I found the sun flirting
with fresh-washed lilac
paint and sheep
silent in their shades.

I found a pride of dandelions
uninvited
yet welcome with their joyous roar
and stars of fire
flashed in the scrub.

I found the track
had been a river
last night and spiders
cast their nets
to catch my morning face.

I found my pants
swished darker   cooler
soaked by the flexing
grass cohering
with my calves and shins.

I found a hole
in my shoe.

I found bracken
fronds unfurling
in homage to Fibonacci.

I found a diligence of ants
bent on reconstruction.

I found parrots posing
on a new blue fence.

And I found goat's
yoghourt —
stringent and spare.

And words
for a poem.

Cloud-sheep

They are shooting
the sheep — so little
noise — a "puh"
and they fall in dust.

☾

The flock rests flat belly
down on the grazing
layer — the long blue
air of its place.

Slide

Two sea-eagles slide
across morning. Each trim
of wing and tail leaves us solid
as stone on the sandy track.

As they fly
into the sun we hold our hands
against blinding. Our breath
against melting wax.

Drought

The dams — mud
rhombuses.

Not even cattle
tracks remain.

A woven
plastic sack

flayed
against barbs

spread —
an eagle

in a flashback
when feathers

flew
and claws dripped

blood.
A grey carcass

slumps
beside its stump

and spotted
gums rise from buff

dust.
And the dams

mere
rhombuses.

Their Words
(*at Hill End*)

The mullock of their words lies heaped
and mute.   The flakes
and rubble of their chatter
scattered.
                    The ground
bears this load
in silence.

As cattle roam the common, the bones
of their speech may stir
and turn; but as I walk
the old mine track, these stones
lie taciturn. The murmuring of mullock
heaps heard only by the wagtails flouncing
there, where skinks tip-tilt alert
their fine bronze heads and snakes
taste the sere and amber rustle of their words

And in the old batteries
their sentences split and seize
with rust and crumble (mashed
and prized with dust and mumble)

Their voices have fallen
deep in holes in the past of this place,
where deeper still abound; the shafts
and adits trivial or profound.

Like bones each crush
and crunch of rock a word
lying white and grey-
veined, flush orange and russet, crimson,
brown and large enough to break a toe
or tooth. And not yet smoothed
by wind and rain; and not yet eased
by time. Their crushed
and jagged syntax lies
at odds — a shout, a secret breathed,
a scream, then whimpering,
swash and boasting,
chipped, abrasive, angular — awkward
underfoot.

When large drops fall
a Hill End summer afternoon, they sigh
at such relief from alien
heat and unrelenting torpor.

The trees are privy
to their words. They probe
and aspirate

White silence

This morning earth's white
whispering of names
embraces all
excludes all.   Tree-
tops fade in the pale
space of sky.   A broken
twig and loosened
leaf float in a prophecy
of falling.   Bird call
is captive to this white
silence.   Suspended words
flow from our lips
to join the morning
earth's white whispering
of names.

Sketches from a garden

it flurries, then melts as it settles
too soon
always too soon

☾

snow-melt reveals a spare thatch of needles
resinous and glowing in early evening

☾

the snapped twig, the fallen leaf, the slew of bark
dust of pollen
dust of dust

☾

in this pool the moon
will be reflected
when the cloud passes

its most pallid face
will wane and stammer
with the plaint of plovers

☾

when the mopoke calls and snails
raise their horns to bellow at the moon

the tallest trees lean near
to hear the sundering of earth

☾

when there is heat
when the wind roars and our ears
fill with the shrieking of orange

beneath all
the imperturbable breathing
of green

☾

when the great winds blow and there is a face
    in every fallen leaf
when the air is filled with the debris of dreams
when the sky greens darkly
when the trees bow before their lashing
    with grace
when birds retreat to the calmer depths
    of the forest
is a time to beat the heart and breathe

☾

The leaves are drying
brown

They flail and furl and fold
and fall with a rattle

And there are the flat
maps of feet

and empty pods
watching.

Kings

The eucalyptus trembles
in a florescence of parrots —
wayward blooms
of emerald, viridian,
scarlet, vermilion.

The morning squints
and shades its eyes
then draws a veil
around itself — against
this clarion sight.

Secreted in mist
the kings have their way
with the tree. Crack
open her fruit, swing crazed
lanterns from her slender limbs.
Torch her.

After a walk to the frog pond

I used to think the rose was my flower
but now yearn for the spare chaste
symmetry of Mitrasacme
(polymorpha).

Bound by the rule of macadam
the rose was soft,
abundant, blowsy,
lush, its colour,

bud and burst
and fall
a respite from grey
orthodoxy.

But here,
where the scrub scrambles
incoherently,
the sign of the small

white quatrefoil advocates
order, its grace
a haven
from bush havoc.

Its clear
white shines
from the scribbled
splatter,

scrape
and scratch —
an unrelenting
Pollock of terrain.

Have you heard?
(Sunday, Adelaide Botanic Gardens)

Have you heard the drying
lotus leaves at the lotus pond
on the second day after the heat —
the desiccated
semaphore, the curling brown?

Have you heard the flat
of green sapped leaves?

Have you heard the echo
of white hands tuned to the light
of the sun?

Heard the children's eyes
snap as they drink last drops
with straws?

Have you heard the plane-
tree scrape the sky?
Heard the blue
frisson, the dappling
of limbs?
Trace
and tremble in the canopy?

Have you heard the unfurling
of ferns, pale writhing
of the toolur[*],   the thin

and peeling skins of paperbarks,
down
on the giant geranium,
the sighing of the dark
and casuarina hair?

Have you heard
the drying of the leaves?

★ Eucalyptus Grandis

The hands of autumn

They lie in the chill path of autumn —
the writhing hands of Grünewald's Christ,
Dürer's devotions,
pink tips of a babe wrenched
from a withering breast.
Once-pliant fingers stiff,
the stalwart competence of wrists
now brittle twigs. Desiccant
fingers rustle, seeking
succour. There is gold
but the colour of blood prevails.

The first of August

The first of August and the wind
is prompt and opportune. We're

underwater, over-air — swirling
whirled, vertiginous.

Trees lash the blue and whip
the clouds to mound and peak

flail faggots for an August
burn of witches

limbs abandoned to the pyre.
The wires wail thin and plaint.

I throw bread but the birds
have withdrawn.

Curl

Leaf
hands
curl
crisp
as dying

as the dying
curl in
on themselves
nails gouge
palms

and palms exude
the carmine sap
of dried
crushed
female
beetles.

Harmonics

Now the trees have fallen
the roar of wind subsides
to the stretched harmonics of the roar
the high-strung strands
the shards of shattered sounds
the click of twigs
the shredded stripped skin wan
the pale limbs wail
while feathers twirl.
The faint faint faint harmonics of the roar
now lost in deep
and silent dust, in falling
flakes of ancient skin and the vagrant
twittering of unhatched chicks.

Winter Cycle

Now we see
the bare beauty of limbs.
After the lashing
one flag remains — red as a sky-wound.
Moss greens and lichens crawl
and beard chill flanks.
From twigs and tips
new worlds invert and shine
and drop
       while we steam out hands
       and stamp.

☾

The sky crackles like a blue tarpaulin.
Nothing comes, nothing
goes. Words rise
vapid on high thermals,
chill as we do, to return
distilled and crystalline.

☾

They rise from the ash of winter — essential
words: hand cup kindness soup
       rug hug ember woodsmoke
       chalice and chocolate and cello.   Others
deep as bears.

☾

The sky is so distant, or is it
closer — hear it
fizz and crack — ice underfoot
a crocus, currawong, a swallow
and its over.

52

Spring in Paris

The first petals almost
an untidyness.   All else
so clearly darkly scribed
austere   precise
pristine   patterned

so   cut
so   shaped
so   cultivated

                    but petals   scrap
and
          scatter
                          (sparely yet)

                                        papers,
butts,
          small   snatches of   something
                                              caught
in the spring
                    afternoon
                                    shift the order
of things;
              hold
                    promise of a

                    loosening
of ties
                    dissolution
                                        of resolution,

nicks
                    in
                    taut
                    membranes.

Blasts shrieks wuthers

No matter how the wind blasts   shrieks
wuthers   there are corners that remain
still   sinister   where truth
holes up.   As children
we made our own wind running to blow away
cobwebs but now they stick.
                    They stick.

The wind inverts words. Benign
intentions turn daft
corners. We collide
with ourselves   eye
for eye   mouth
full of forks.   Truths spear
each day and the innocent
lie bleeding
a flood the wind will never dry.

The cry of the plover

The cry of the plover summons
obscure ghosts   goads
them to hover on the verge
of remembrance   some one
or thing   some time or place
never quite settling   the birds
themselves unsure when
the next cry will tear from their throats
at the uncertain selvedge
of the day   unpick the seams
of sleep   rupture the sack
of sanity.

Night

Sleep has eloped with sanity, fled
from the churning of hours
        (the cold moon white
          on hands and leaves)

The clock no longer ticks and turns. Each minute
melts through the silent shaping of the next
        (the chill moon, stark
          under roofs and eaves)

The world slants with moonlight
where snails track lustre on
the way of dreams
        (the night is cold
          the night is old)

The moon reveals and the tide leaves
too much. Sand
sets like stone.
        (the night is bright
          the night is chill)

The moon wanes and stammers
to the shore. A crab
stitches its reputation across pale mounds.

The stones affirm our destiny.
        (the waves hush
          the waves hush
          the waves hush)

Raven

*a glossy blue-
black crow of the genus
Corvus*

The ravenous dark
plunders all sounds
but heartbeat

amplifies the crimson
and gelatinous thud
of carrion.

Black cherry
jam drying
on fingers

will not be
washed with any
but blood-

hot water
and the pit
clicks cleaned

of its flesh
on the plate
affirming

promise
of unimagined
lightness.

Even the words
(*dirge*)

The word tastes of ash
all words
(all things) taste
of ash

ash in shades
of grey with the feel
of grit between
teeth

tree tastes of ash
leaf tastes of ash
bark tastes of ash
grass tastes of ash

house car
bike trike stroller
all ash
in the mouth

man and woman
and child and babe
horse and cow
dog and cat and bird

rose and thorn
house and home
cup and knife
table and bed

bread and butter
and honey and jam
cheese and milk
and strawberries and cream

snake and lizard
bird and bat
wombat and mouse
grub and moth

skin and kin
and hair and fur
and feather taste
of ash

courage and fear
and even rose
taste
of ash

We need new flowers
(*dirge*)

We need new flowers.
If there were roses, now they all
are stones. The earth groans with the weight
of such transformations.

A child throws a stone
a mother weeps
her tears are red petals
they stain the earth
no rain will fall to cleanse it

a youth straps into his bomb
words warp in the heat
they set as stones in blistered mouths
unkindness knows no bounds

an old man hobbles across raw earth
his hands are open
his eyes are closed against the bleeding of so many
stones
his tears the only rain
his hands are open
he seeks a home
there is no home
his hands are open
his mother is a stone
his father is a stone
his wife is a stone

his son is a stone
his daughter is a stone
his cousins his uncles his aunts
are stones
they are all
stones

all the mothers
all the fathers
all the sons
all the daughters
all the uncles the aunts the cousins
all the grandparents
all the yet unborn
are stones

there is nothing but stones
even the roses
are stones and the stones
have the smell of iron.

Kafkaesque

Kafka has hijacked the beetles. Turned
summer nights to a sorry orgy.
Each crisp-cased coracle waves
lilliputian
demanding
rescue.   Gulliver — my fingers
fumble on Gregor's smooth
wing-case, turn him with care
for tiny legs and tiny clinging claws.
Mind now! No matter —
one of his six legs stumbles and flip
he's over again, and waving. Padding
barefoot in the hot dark night for water
death cracks beneath my feet.

Sunday morning

The currawongs this morning
sing such a chorus of joy
we will try to ignore
the flaying and the shedding
and look into the timeless lucid
blue with steadfast gaze
and rejoice that our fingers
still chill pink
at the tips
while the few remaining leaves
flag the hue
and cry of blood.

Something

There was something about the way
they held their hands, as though
they had only now become aware of these
obscure and fleshly rectangles
appended to the stumps of their arms.

In their waking — the words
were never there.   Only fingers
testing the air between them and finding
it chill against the webbing.

Paper, candle, moon

A paper boat floats

           under a spattering of gnats

The candle glows

           but does not burn

Water seeps

           but does not soak.

The moon rocks and croons

           as it watches itself.

There are no more hands

           to fold paper.

Easter morning

Easter morning
Bach's Passion
surges through the house.

On the table with chocolate
Easter eggs, ten gerberas rise
on sinuous green stems.

Every flower is a wound.
The petals splash blood
from their appalling eyes.

We are watched
by wounds. Always
by wounds.

Here is an Easter
feast of fruity buns
and fragrant coffee.

The news is that
the wounding
has not stopped.

Poppies

The poppies writhe
as they approach
their unsealing.
Each bud is green and each
hair curves to thoughts
of wax and blades.

One hints
one smiles
one blushes
as its pink
protrudes from hirsute
calyces.

(My lips read the breath-
misted braille of fine finger
hairs as the pen pauses
at my mouth seeking
word shape.)

I have not brushed the poppies'
lips with mine; they are
too green, too like
the sweaty shaven
legs of cyclists, underarms, a week-old
bikini-line, lips

after childbirth.
The furred and tender
buds swell secretly

then part in measured
peeling back of green and hairy
lips round a mouth-

full and filling,
folded, furled
their substance
blushing pink
blazing
cadmium — yellow, orange,
scarlet.

These mouths
when flames are blown
curl back to crisp
and fall (dust
of green lips).

Pensées

The eleven black pansies I planted for you
no longer bloom. Pallid —
they stuttered and waned in bright sun
glowed lurid in the darkest hours
then dropped.

Your face hovers.
A fallen petal lies beneath my feet.
Cracks appear.
The earth gives up
the smell of last night's rain.

Remembering Mother's Birthday
(*Mollymook*)

slow
moves the mollusk
one
grain
at a time

(the birds
are from a different tribe)

sun on my left cheek
sun on my right

once more
a single
tear evaporates

Rustle

I know there are still
flakes of you
in the corners of this room.
I hear them rustle
each time I enter. They recall
the quaver of your voice.
The cat twitches
her ears. I sneeze against a hint
of ancient talc, a lingering whiff
of stale cologne. The wisp
of a single hair uncurls —
bent on discomposure —
a tissue in the pocket
of a gown you wore — your juices
dried.

Red and crisp

The apple is red
and crisp. Snaps.
         (the currawongs await the core)
The air is crisp.
The last leaves flare and crackle, flaunt
their red. Fingers
bleed on the page.
Weep at such razor redness.

Crisp and red the words
that pass between us, others
chewed to the core. Do apples
bleed as we bite them, slice them
to excise the worm? Do they
lament their wasted
seed? While I wonder, red
words stab — deep
and crisp and even.

Smudge

Tell me how it was.
Erasure has left mere smudges.
Lines lack distinction, colours drab,
the dark is ash, the light subdued by shades
My ears are plugged with the silt of amnesia
the timbre of each moment muffed.

Tell me how it was.

Of course there are memorable blots,
variously read according to moon or tide.
Cicatrix worth counting, bruises
which will never fade, fissures and gobbets,
barnacles and folds
still warm. Still intimate. But tell me
again
how it was.

The stones

The stones are taciturn
dependable
their edge and rounding warm
beneath my feet   though briefly
wave-washed cool

                              night
and the storm rumbles
boulders   hurls
mass against mass
                            crack
against crack

fissures appear in sleep
dreams rupture

(the muttering of marbles
in a sack)

now morning calms
kelp-chill and pungent feet
                          falter
as the weed dries
                          warps
and waits
to lacerate

The stones are taciturn
dependable.

On the track

The afternoon clatters
with dropped names.
                        On the pavement
against ambitious glass and steel
they peal.   Reverberate.
                        But on the track
our footfall soft as dust
absorbs all acclamation.
                        The stones remain
unmoved.   Trees
yield to the wind, and the leaves and grasses
whisper unpretentiously.
                        I observe
the integrating industry of ants pushing
their grains of sand to modest heights.
                        The wallaby
will leave its honest shit
on the track again tonight.

The tacit truth of stone

The flower drops heavy
as a head.

The petals spread
like tongues — pink

pliant and murmuring
still. Lips and eye-

lids close or gape;
flutter, fade and wane

before the tacit
truth of stone.

Present in the morning

To answer
present in the morning
presence of light
        on earth
        on grass
        on tree
on rock and house
on leaf and bird,
to see
a world
illumined
is to know
for this day
one is,
amid such presences.

To see
the frosted white
to feel
the pinking chill of finger
rose of cheek dew
softened,
to see our
breathing
balloon
into the morning
is to know
for this day

one breathes
the world that breathes all
things as names.

To hear
you say my name
and answer
present in the morning
is to know
that we
are here, each
with the other
and the breathing
of the world in
names   of earth
          of grass
          of tree
of rock and house
of leaf and bird.

The typeface of this book is the work of NICOLAS JENSON (1420-1480), engraver, printer and type designer. This font, named after Jenson, first appeared in 1470 in Venice, and is still admired as one of the finest of all type-designs. William Morris praised the beauty and perfection of this roman font.